Where We Worship

Muslim
Mosque

Angela Gluck Wood

W
FRANKLIN WATTS
LONDON • SYDNEY

This is one of the symbols used to represent Islam, the religion of Muslims.

When a Muslim uses the name of Allah or the Prophet Muhammad, they show respect by saying, 'Peace and blessings be upon him'.

For Rizwaan and Maleeha Malik

This edition first published 2005

Franklin Watts
96 Leonard Street
London EC2A 4XD

Franklin Watts Australia
45-51 Huntley Street
Alexandria NSW 2015

© Franklin Watts 1998

Editor: Samantha Armstrong
Series Designer: Kirstie Billingham
Illustrator: Gemini Patel
Religious Education Consultant: Margaret Barratt MA, Religious Education Lecturer and author
Religious Consultant: Mr Nazar-e Mustafa, Education Consultant, Central London Mosque
Reading Consultant: Prue Goodwin, Reading and Literacy Centre, Reading

Dewey Decimal Classification Number 297

A CIP catalogue record for this book is available from
the British Library

ISBN 0 7496 6204 2

Printed in China

Contents

Mosques around the world

Mosques are places where Muslims meet to study and pray to God. Muslims also pray at home.

There are mosques ▷ all over the world. This one is in England.

Muslim beliefs

Muslims believe that there is only one God, called **Allah.** Allah sent an angel, Gabriel, to a man named **Muhammad** who lived in Saudi Arabia. The angel told Muhammad that Allah wanted him to be his messenger or **prophet.** Muhammad was told by Gabriel what Allah wanted him to teach others.

There are no ▷ pictures or statues of Allah or the Prophet Muhammad inside a mosque. Instead the walls and ceilings are decorated with beautiful patterns and writing.

Prayer times

Muslims can go to the mosque at any time but midday on Friday is especially important. Muslims pray five times a day. The exact times of prayers change through the year.

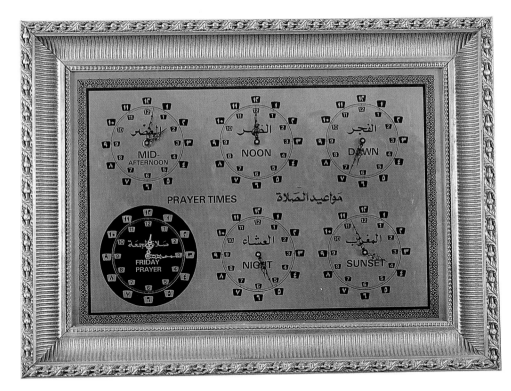

▲ Many mosques have clock boards showing the prayer times for each day. The clocks start at the top on the right. The dark clock shows the time for the prayers at midday on Friday.

8

The call to prayer

When it is time to pray a man calls out from a **minaret** or tower on the mosque. He is called a **muezzin.** Sometimes the call to prayer is played through a speaker.

This is a muezzin calling ▷ people to prayer. In some countries the call is broadcast on the television and radio.

The Ka'aba

Muslims always face the same way when they pray. They face towards a building called the **Ka'aba.** The Ka'aba is in the city of **Makkah** in Saudi Arabia. The very first offering made to Allah was at the Ka'aba.

The Prophet Muhammad lived in Makkah and taught people the important messages he had from Allah.

◁This is a model of the cube-shaped Ka'aba.

Muslims try to visit ▷
Makkah at least once. This special visit is called Hajj.

10

Inside a mosque

The main part of a mosque is the **prayer hall**.
There is no furniture in the hall
but there are carpets or mats to pray on.
Men and women pray separately.

Here Muslim men ▷
are praying together.
The carpets help them
to stay in straight lines.

Inside every mosque are copies of the **Qur'an**.
The Qur'an is the special book
for Muslims. It is written in **Arabic**.
Everything that Allah told to the
Prophet Muhammad is written in the Qur'an.
It is treated with love and respect.

◀ Muslims try to learn the Qur'an by heart.

The Qur'an is placed on a stand ▶ to keep it clean and to show how important it is.

14

The mihrab and minbar

Every mosque has a place on one wall, called a **mihrab.** This shows the direction (**qiblah**) of the Ka'aba. Near the mihrab there is a platform called a **minbar.** This is where the **imam,** or prayer leader, stands every Friday at midday when he speaks to the people.

▷ Here the mihrab and minbar are together in the mosque. The imam is standing on the minbar facing the people.

◁ This is a minbar on its own.

16

Getting ready to pray

When Muslims go into a mosque, they take off their shoes. This is to show their **respect**. Then they wash carefully.

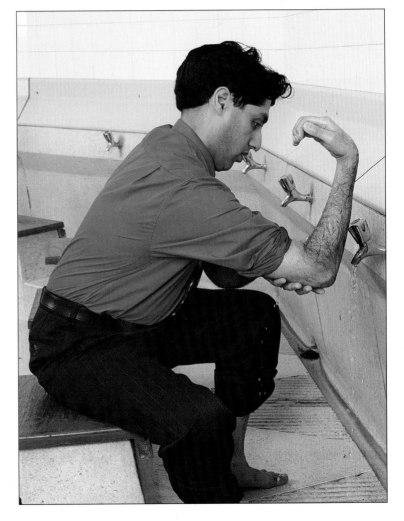

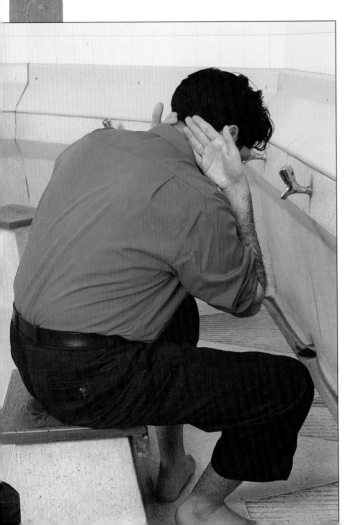

It is important to be very clean to pray to Allah. Before Muslims wash they think of Allah.

There is an order for washing. First Muslims wash their hands. Then they wash their mouth, nose, face and arms.

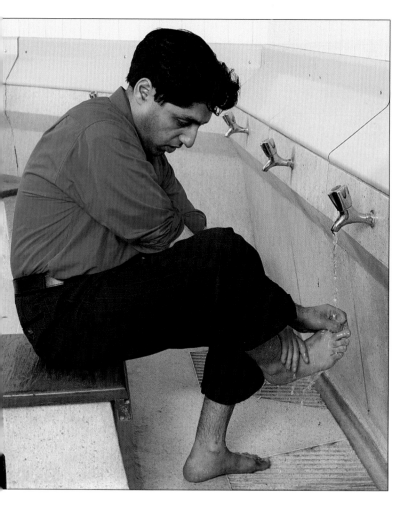

Next they wash their head, neck and ears. Lastly they wash their feet. The washing is called **wudu**.

Prayer positions

Muslims pray with their whole bodies. They use ten different positions. Altogether the positions are called a **rak'ah**.

◀ ▼ ▶ Three positions are shown here.

By bending and bowing until their forehead is on the ground, Muslims show how great Allah is. At the same time, they say 'Allahu Akbar' which means 'Allah is the Greatest'.

Muslim dress

It is important for Muslims to dress in a way that shows their respect for Allah. Their clothes cover their bodies from their neck to their ankles.

Some Muslim ▷ girls and women keep their heads covered at all times. Here a group of Muslim girls are praying together.

Helping others

Many mosques have a collection box. Muslims believe that they should help other people as much as they can. One way they do this is to give money to charity. This is called **sadaqah**. Doing good things is sadaqah too.

Once a year every family is also asked to pay money to help poorer people. This is called **zakah.**

This boy is putting ▷ money in the collection box at the mosque.

A school in a mosque

Most mosques have classes for children at weekends or after school.
The children are taught how to lead a Muslim way of life. They also read the Qur'an and try to learn it by heart.

When they are young boys and girls study together. When they are older, they have separate classes.

Here a group of ▷
Muslim girls
are learning Arabic.

Glossary

Allah   the Muslim name for God

Arabic   the language spoken in Saudi Arabia. The Qur'an is written in Arabic

imam   the person who leads the prayers in the mosque

Ka'aba   the cube-shaped building in Makkah. Muslims pray in the direction of the Ka'aba

Makkah   the city in Saudi Arabia where the Prophet Muhammad was born. Muslims try to go to Makkah at least once in their lives

mihrab   a place on the wall of the prayer hall that shows the direction for prayer

minaret   the tower on or near a mosque that is used to call Muslims to prayer

minbar   a short staircase with a platform on top where the imam stands to talk to the people

mosque	the place where Muslims meet to study and pray together
muezzin	the person who calls Muslims to prayer. (It is also written as muadhin.)
prayer hall	the room in the mosque where Muslims pray
prophet	a messenger for God. Muhammad is the Prophet of Allah
qiblah	the direction of the Ka'aba
Qu'ran	the Muslim holy book
rak'ah	a set of positions for prayer
respect	to treat well
sadaqah	charity
wudu	washing before prayer
zakah	paying money for poor people once a year

Index

Photographic acknowledgements:
Cover: Steve Shott Photography
Insides P6 Hutchison
P7 H. Rogers, Trip

P9 Christine Osborne
P11 Trip
P23 Abbas/Magnum
P27 Abbas/Magnum

All other photographs are by
Steve Shott Photography
With thanks to the East London Mosque
and the Central London Mosque